WHEN THE TIME IS RIGHT, MOVE ON

FAYE E. J. THOMAS

ISBN: 0-7596-6947-3

This book is printed on acid free paper.

1stBooks - rev. 04/29/02

CONTENTS

CHAPTER 1

IN THE BEGINNING

On a beautiful summer day in Summerfield, Louisiana, my grandmother Allie and some women in the community had planned a fishing trip to Little Corner Bottom, but I interrupted their plans that day. It was a hot steamy day in August that I decided to see what the outside world had in store for me.

My mother and father were living with my grandparents, Allie and John Hunter, at the time that I was born. Therefore, Mother Hunter and her fishing friends decided to cancel their fishing trip and wait until I made by appearance. Mrs. Addie Phillips, a midwife, (as women who deliver babies are called) was summoned to help with my arrival. As they waited, socialized, ate lunch, ate dinner and waited several more hours, I finally made my appearance.

Cousin Vera Allen named me Faye Evelyn. She had seen a movie actress with that name. Unfortunately, I never had the opportunity to see the movie star from whom my name was chosen.

I was a welcomed newcomer to the community of Summerfield, Louisiana in 1933. During that time, there was the great depression. I have frequently heard my grandparents talk about the difficult times that people experienced during the depression with Herbert Hoover as president of the United States.

The economic, agricultural, and relief policies under the administration of President Franklin D. Roosevelt did a great deal to improve the effects of the depression.

As economic conditions improved, my parents moved into a house on Grandfather Johnson's farm where my father worked as a sharecropper with his father. He farmed until I was four years old. After the farming experience, he did what was known as public work. Public work consisted of cutting trees for logs that were used to make furniture and paper.

During our early childhood, my brother (fifteen months younger than I am) and I enjoyed visiting our grandparents, John and Allie Hunter, and Will and Olelia Johnson. We also enjoyed two great grandmothers, Great grandmother Mary Ann and Great grandmother Isabell. They both had very unique personalities and they were very strong church-going and God-fearing women.

DEDICATION

This book is dedicated to my family:

Mother--------------Altee Johnson

Son------------------Dwayne Buggs

Brothers ------------John W. Johnson, Sr.
Steve Johnson

Sisters --------------Alicia Lemoins
Bonnie G. Johnson

Aunt ----------------Esther Nelson

Thanks for the inspiration, wisdom, and encouragement that you expressed in all of my endeavors.

ACKNOWLEDGMENT

Many people have taught me through the years that when the time is right, move on. When I finished high school, the time was right for me to leave my parents and brother and go to college. When I graduated from college, the time was right for me to begin my family and pursue my career. As circumstances and events entered in and out of my life, I moved on when the time was right for me.

I am grateful to Suren for encouraging me to write this book. Thanks to Leroy for listening to me talk about my writing. I appreciate Margaret Redmond and Marilyn Okoye for their support and encouragement during this writing process.

Thanks to my son, Dwayne, for the long distance telephone calls and to Marilyn for advising me how to use the computer.

My sincere appreciation is extended to Nancy Zemek for designing the book cover.

CHAPTER 2

SUMMERFIELD

Summerfield is a rural area in the northern section of Louisiana. The population was about 400 during the World War 1 and World War 11 timeline. The economy was poor. People farmed on a small scale and cut pulp wood. However, the above average White woman had a maid to help with house work. It was the Black woman who served as maid. The average family of six in a household raised three or four bales of cotton, corn, sweet potatoes, hogs, cows, farm animals- horses, mules, small domestic animals-chickens, dogs, cats, etc. Many families had vegetable gardens and flower gardens.

There were churches scattered around the area. My family attended Mt. Calm Baptist Church, Mt. Olive Baptist Church, and sometimes, on special occasions, Fellowship Baptist Church.

There were schools for children in grades pre-primer through seventh grade for African Americans. The school consisted of one large room, one teacher with children in each grade.

When children finished the seventh grade, they had to go to other communities for high school studies, even though, there was a high school in their community. It was restricted to Whites. Some of the children went to Fellowship High School, Bernice, and Homer High School. Many continued their education at Grambling State University and Southern University.

Social activities were very limited. There were no museums, theaters, or recreational centers. However, there was a bar "across the creek", called "On the Hill", where some adults would go on Saturday nights, drink beer and listen to music by popular singers on the juke box.

There were three very talented men in the community who could play excellent music with their harmonica, fiddle, and guitar. They were great entertainers at house parties. Instead of going "On the Hill", some people would go to house parties to listen to the harmonica, guitar, and fiddle players.

Other forms of entertainment were baseball games and turkey shoots. The turkey was not actually shot. If an individual could hit the target, he would receive a turkey.

There was one doctor in Summerfield. Dr. Algood would see patients in his office and he would also make house calls.

Mrs. Ethel Raley served as a cab driver for many people in the community. She would take them places for a small fee.

Thus, life in Summerfield continues today with many changes that were brought about through the years.

Early history revealed that Summerfield was situated in the Northwestern portion of Claiborne Parish. It was settled by W. R. Kennedy in 1868, by the erection of a wood and blacksmith shop, and a business house. It had four stores dealing in general merchandise and plantation supplies, several drug stores, a saw and grist mill, and several mills in the vicinity run by steam. There were four churches, M.E. Church South, Methodist, Protestant, Missionary Baptist and Primitive Baptist. The town had a school building. Mail delivery was twice a week.

The country surrounding Summerfield was in prosperous condition, with good water, pure air, and fertile soil. The land was well timbered, and could be purchased at a price of one to five dollars per acre.

The agricultural future was bright for those who wanted to do farm work. Therefore, some of my ancestors settled in Summerfield.

This early description of Summerfield was presented in THE HISTORY OF CLAIBORNE PARISH that was compiled by D. W. Harris and Hulse.

CHAPTER 3

OLD TIME REVIVAL

Once a year, usually during the summer, churches would have an "Old Time Revival". Revival meeting would start on Sunday and end on Friday night. In the announcement about the revival, it was stated that "Dinner will be on the ground". Community people knew exactly what that meant. Families would bring large boxes of food to be served after the morning service. Tables would be set up outside of the church under the shade of trees. The women would set their boxes of food on the tables, and everyone would be served.

My brother John and I would eat only our grandparents' food of which our mother would have helped to prepare. You would never dream of such a feast. There would be fried chicken, chicken and dressing, roast beef, ham, pork chops, sweet potato pie, lemon pie, chocolate pie, fried apple pies, pound cake, coconut cake, pineapple cake, potato salad, fruit salad, peas, string beans, collard greens, rolls, and corn bread. This would be served during the break between morning service and afternoon service.

Near the end of the day, everyone would return to their homes satisfied with the church service and the "Dinner on the Ground".

Monday through Friday, revival would be held at night. My family would end their work early, get dressed, and rush to get to Mt. Calm or Mt. Olive Baptist churches in time for the beginning of the service.

Devotion, which consisted of singing hymns and praying preceded the pastor's sermon. Children who were not members of the church would sit on the front pew facing the altar until they became members.

Great Grandmother Mary Ann Hunter would be requested to pray every night. I suppose she was requested to pray because her prayers were long and well-worded. After praying for about fifteen minutes, she would end her prayer with the following words: Oh Lord, please bless the offsprings of my body. There are some in this world, I know not where they are. Oh Lord, please take care of me, and when it is my time to go, and yours to stay, come on into my dying room, and press a dying pillow under my head. Help me to die. Show me how to die in peace of all mankind, for ever, Amen."

My brother John and I continued to sit on that front pew, along with others, of course. The minister preached and preached about heaven and hell. The doors of the church were opened each night for new membership. Finally, on Friday night, the doors of the church were opened again for new members. My brother John walked up and shook the pastor's hand. The pastor asked John to make a statement. He said, "I came to join the church. I want to be baptized. I feel like the Lord has pardoned my sins." Thus, he became a member of the church that night. I continued to sit on the front pew. When I got home I thought about it. If my brother was going to be a christian, and I am older than he, I want to be a christian, too. Therefore, I told my grandfather, Deacon Will Johnson, that I wanted to be baptized. Thus, Grandfather informed the pastor, Reverend Rutland, who was spending the night with my grandparents, that I wanted to be baptized. Reverend Rutland asked me a few questions about why I wanted to be baptized. My answers were accepted; however, I did not tell him that it was because my brother was being baptized. Therefore, my brother and I were baptized on the same day in the beautiful clear spring water that flowed into the baptizing pond near where my grandparents lived.

CHAPTER 4

THE GREAT STORYTELLER

When my brother John and I were about 3 and 4 years of age, we were introduced to the printed words. My parents subscribed to the Shreveport Journal newspaper and Progressive Farmer magazine. We were read to frequently. Mother is very creative. She used the newspaper for different purposes. The valentine that I will always remember is the one that she made from newspaper on Valentine day when I was four years old. My brother and I would not have been more excited it she had purchased them from a store.

We would jump up and down when our parents would say, "You will spend the afternoon with Grandpa John Lowery." We knew that we would be entertained all afternoon. Grandpa John Lowery had books galore, we thought. As I think about it today, there were probably no more than twelve books on his bookshelf. He would read and tell us stories. We heard all about "Brother Rabbit", "The Three Little Pigs", The Fox and the Sour Grapes", "The Tiger That Turned Into Butter", and many

11

other stories. Sometimes, he would let us choose a book for him to read. Of course, we chose books according to the pictures in them.

Many times we would have Grandpa to repeat a story that he had previously told us. At the end of the afternoon, I am sure that he was glad for our parents to take us home. He has always been remembered as the greatest storyteller.

Then, one day, Grandpa Lowery became ill. On the way to a hospital, the driver had an automobile accident, and Grandpa died in the accident. We grieved his death, but we never forgot the great storyteller.

CHAPTER 5

THE ACAPPELLA SINGERS

On cold winter nights in the Mt. Olive community where Grandfather John Hunter and Grandmother Allie Hunter lived, singing was a form of entertainment.

Our mother was their only child; therefore, my brother and I referred to our grandparents as Mother Hunter and Daddy Hunter.

Daddy Hunter would say, "We had better get our night work done." The night work which started about six o'clock in the evening consisted of milking the cows, feeding the hogs, horses, cattle and chickens.

After the night work was finished, we would sit down at the long dining room table for supper that Mother Hunter had prepared. I often wondered why they needed a dining room table that was so long. Later, I realized that they would frequently have visitors and relatives who filled the twelve chairs around the table.

Before eating a parcel of food, we, individually, had to say a Bible verse. My brother and I would say the shortest one, "Jesus wept." Daddy Hunter, who was a very humorous man, would add to our verses by saying: "Jesus wept, Moses slept, and I fell out of the back door steps." After we had eaten and the dishes had been washed, we would go into the sitting room, which consisted of two full size beds, dresser and chairs. Mother Hunter believed in having enough beds. She had four bedrooms and six full size beds.

We would sit around the fireplace of which Daddy Hunter had built a fire that would light up the room. He would get the songbooks. He and Mother Hunter would sing songs from those books without musical accompaniment. They would sing "I'll Fly Away", "The Lord Will Make A way", and many other songs.

On Sunday mornings, Daddy Hunter would take his songbooks to church, because he knew that he and Mother Hunter would be requested to sing. Two of their favorite songs were: "I'll Fly Away" and "The Lord will make a Way Somehow." The words are too precious to omit.

I'll Fly Away
Albert E. Brumley

Some glad morning when this life is o'er—I'll fly
away
To a home on God's celestial shore.
Refrain: I'll fly away, fly away, fly away-In the
Morning-when I die hal-le-lu-jah, by and by
I'll fly away.

When the shadows of this life have grown, I'll fly
away.
Like a bird from prison walls has flown, I'll fly
away.

The Lord Will Make A Way Somehow

Like a ship that's tossed and driven
Battered by an angry sea,
When the storms of life are raging,
And their fury falls on me,
I wonder what I have done,
That makes this race so hard to run,
Then I'll say to my courage, take courage.
The lord will make a way somehow.

Chorus: The Lord will make a way somehow,
When beneath the cross I bow,
He will take away each sorrow.
Let Him have your burdens now.
When the load bears down so heavy,
The weight is shown upon my brow.
There is a sweet relief in knowing,
O the Lord will make a way somehow.

I have heard Mother Hunter and Daddy Hunter sing those songs numerous times. Therefore, my brother and I grew up with the idea that God will make a way, and that idea became a reality in our lives.

CHAPTER 6

CULLEN U.S.A.

My father decided that he wanted to improve his economic condition. Therefore, he went to a small paper mill town, about forty miles northwest from where we lived, and got a job at Southern Kraft paper mill.

Having worked at the paper mill six weeks, he decided to move his family, which consisted of my mother, brother, and me. I was excited because we were moving to a town where the population was larger than our country area. The time was right, so we moved to Cullen, Louisiana.

We packed our clothes, furniture, and said, "Good-bye" to our grandparents and friends. We rode for an hour over gravel, bumpy road. Finally, we arrived at our two-bedroom apartment. We met the owner who had a very unique personality. Each morning she would sprinkle salt on the doorsteps. "We had never seen anyone sprinkle salt on door steps. We asked, "Why is she sprinkling salt?" My mother said that she probably does that to get rid of evil spirits, or for some other superstitious reasons.

We stayed at that apartment about six months. Then, my father rented a house on a well-kept street where all the houses were made alike and painted white. He was in walking distance of his work and my brother and I were in walking distance of the school. Even though my father had an automobile, he did not drive it to work.

We looked forward to Thursdays because that was payday for my father. He would get his check cashed, pay the rent, which was $2.50 per week, give my mother money to buy food, and pay the electricity and gas bills.

On Saturdays, Daddy would give my brother and me fifty cents. My friends, who had fifty cents, and I would go to Springhill, which was two miles away, to the movie theaters. The fifty cents enabled me to ride the 10 cents bus to and from Springhill, pay twelve cents admission to the State Theater, and nine cents admission to the Webster Theater. That left me nine cents to buy pop or candy.

The theaters were segregated, as well as restaurants, buses, trains, restrooms, churches, and schools in the South. African Americans had to sit on the second level at the theaters, whereas, the

Caucasians sat on the first level. That was the custom at the time, but I enjoyed climbing upstairs to see a good movie starring Rock Hudson, John Wayne, and others.

There were times, instead of buying pop or candy, we'd go to the drug store and buy an ice cream cone. Blacks were not allowed to sit inside at the counter and eat the ice cream. The seats were reserved for White people. Therefore, some of us would stand at the end of the counter, purchase the ice cream and walk outside to eat it. That was the way of life in the South during the 1940's.

Cullen was divided into two sections for Blacks and Whites. The section where most of the Blacks lived was called "Froggy Bottom". In Froggy Bottom, African Americans owned grocery stores, furniture stores, barbershops, beauty shops, taxicabs, restaurants, and several bars where beer and liquor were sold.

Thursday nights, Friday nights, and Saturday nights were very lively in Froggy Bottom. Men who worked at the paper mill were paid on Thursdays, other workers were paid on Fridays, and pulp wood and saw mill workers were paid on Saturdays. Therefore, parties would start on Thursday night and end on Saturday night for some people. Several people lost their lives or became injured as a result of the action that took place in the "Bottom".

People from surrounding areas near and far would come to Froggy Bottom for large gambling games. Men with long shiny cars would gather with pockets of money to play the card game for three days in succession. Some men would bring their women with them. Others would find one in the Bottom. Thus, you can see that there was plenty action in Froggy Bottom.

CHAPTER 7

SCHOOL DAYS

I was a happy first grader at Mt. Calm School in Summerfield, Louisiana. I quickly learned to read and memorize things. One of the songs that I memorized for a Christmas program was "Christmas Is Coming". The words were as follows:

Christmas is coming,
The goose is getting fat.
Please put a penny
In the old man's hat.

I knew the words, therefore, during practice, I was singing loud, long, and perhaps wrong. My teacher scolded me severely and said that she would tell my mother about my singing. That ended my singing career before I got started. As a result of that experience, I have never sung in school choirs or church choirs. My mother said, "I wish that teacher had told me about your singing.

I would have had news for her." I am sure that it would not have been good news.

During my second grade year, I appeared on a program reciting this poem:

Steaming Water
Watch the steaming water,
Coming from the pot.
Steam is on the water
That is very hot.

At the end of my third grade year in Summerfield, I found that I had to repeat it because I had missed 20 days of school due to having asthma.

I entered Cullen Elementary School in third grade. The school consisted of four rooms and three teachers. At the end of that year, I was promoted to fourth grade. Fourth and fifth graders were in different sections of the same classroom. The teacher would write fourth and fifth grade assignments on the chalkboard, I would do both assignments. Therefore, the teacher decided to let me do fifth grade work. At the end of the year, I was promoted to the sixth grade. Well, the following year, I was in the classroom with sixth and seventh graders. I again did the work of both grades. At the end of six weeks, the teacher had me to do seventh grade work. When the school year ended, I was promoted to eighth grade. I was happy that I had made two grades in one year twice, but my parents were a little skeptical because I was only eleven years old, almost twelve, and ready to enter high school.

My parents were also concerned that I would have to leave home to enter a high school. There was a high school in my area, but it was for White children. Black children could not attend that school.

Well, my parents took me to Haynesville, Louisiana. They got a room for me with a very kind lady whose husband was in the U.S. Army.

I entered eighth grade at Haynesville Colored High School. After the first semester, my landlady's husband came from the Army. He had served his patriotic time. I could have continued to live with them, but their house was very small. I moved next door and got a room with a very old lady who we called Aunt Rachel Barker. Aunt Rachel was a woman with strong religious traits and character. There were two other girls and a teacher who also rented rooms from Aunt Rachel. Aunt Rachel did not allow the girls to have visitors, especially boys. She would stop them at the gate of her yard, and have them to leave.

The next year I was in the ninth grade. My parents carried me back to Haynesville and got me a room with the Kendrick family. Mr. and Mrs. Kendrick treated me as if I were one of their own children. They had a daughter who was a teacher at the school that I attended and two sons who were in the U.S. Army. They considered me as their little sister. Mrs. Lula Kendrick was a teacher at one of the elementary schools in the parish. Her husband worked on his farm, and was a deacon at Friendship Baptist Church in Haynesville.

I enjoyed staying with them, but I looked forward to Friday evenings. My father would come for me every Friday evening so I could spend the weekends at home. He would take me back on Monday mornings in time for school. Then, he would rush back to his job at the paper mill.

One Friday afternoon, my father had to work overtime. He told me to ride the Trailway bus home. I boarded the bus in Haynesville and sat on one of the seats in the last two rows on the bus, where Blacks were told to sit. I had to change buses in Minden, Louisiana. When I arrived in Minden, the bus to Cullen had gone. Therefore, I was stranded. A porter, working at the bus station, pretended to be nice to me (a little naïve girl), said, "You can spend the night with my mother and get the bus in the morning, but you will have to sleep with me". I said, "No thank you". I got a taxi to take me the 36 miles home. I did not have the money to pay the taxi driver. All the way home, I kept thinking, what will I do if my parents are not home? The taxi driver had stated that the fare would be eight dollars. We arrived in Cullen and I directed the taxi driver to our house. True, to my thinking, my parents were not at home. The taxi driver did not appear to be uneasy about getting his money. I suppose he would have waited until my parents got home.

Mrs. Ida Oliver, one of our neighbors who lived across the street, saw the taxi from Minden in our driveway. She came over and asked the driver how much did he charge for bringing me home. The driver told her that the fare was eight dollars. She paid him. I was happy and I am sure that the taxi driver was too.

My parents had been to the bus station looking for me. When they arrived home, they reimbursed Mrs. Oliver for paying the taxi driver. That was during the time when the neighborhood helped to rear children.

At the end of that school year in Haynesville, I was promoted to tenth grade. I went home for the summer. During that summer, a group of citizens took a petition to the Webster Parish School Board and requested a school bus to take high school children from North Webster Parish to Webster High School in Minden daily. The Webster Parish School Board members decided to honor the citizens' request. They agreed to have a school bus to take African American high school children to the only high school for Blacks in the parish at that time. They called the process "Separate but Equal".

In order to get to this high school for Blacks, we had to leave home about 6:00 in the morning, ride 36 miles one way, pass four high schools for White children, and return home about 6:30 in the evening.

During football season, the bus driver had to wait for football players to finish practice before we could leave for home. One advantage was that the library remained open and we could do our homework during football practice. That year passed successfully. I was promoted to eleventh grade.

Again, citizens were working in the North Webster Parish communities to get a high school for Blacks. A high school was built in Springhill, Louisiana. This school was located two miles from where I lived. Therefore, I was able to finish 11th and 12th grades at Springhill Colored High School. The name of the school was later changed to Charles Brown High School in honor of the first principal, Charles H. Brown.

During my last two years in high school, Miss Essie Youngblood, the librarian, insisted that we learn the contributions of African Americans, which included Marian Anderson, Langston Hughes, Countee Cullen, Lena Horne, Booker T. Washington, Roland Hayes, Althea Gipson, Carter G. Woodson, George Washington Carver, Mary McLeon Bethune, Madam C.J. Walker, Frederick Douglass, Phillis Wheatley, and others.

Each year, a week, Negro History Week, was set aside to celebrate the contributions of African Americans. There would be programs at school as well as at church to honor the contributions of Blacks that were not listed in history books at that time.

Much credit has been given to Carter G. Woodson as founder of Black History Week, which has been extended to Black History Month. During the month of February, recognition is given to African Americans in the areas of sports, music, drama, medicine, science, religion, inventions, engineering, and the list goes on.

Finally, the time came for me to graduate from high school. I was given the honor of presenting the valedictory address. I was proud to be ranked as number one in my very small class.

During my senior year in high school, some of my classmates and I made plans to attend college. I chose to attend Southern University in Baton Rouge and others chose Grambling State University.

To convince my father that I really wanted to attend college, I talked about it a great deal, and I worked at Collie Webb's Memorial Funeral Home that summer following graduation from high school. I served as a receptionist. As a result of working that summer, I was able to buy luggage and some of the clothes that I needed. Thus, my father was convinced that I really wanted to go to college.

In early September of 1950, I packed my clothes that I was taking to college. My parents took me to Minden to get the train to Baton Rouge. At the train station, I was glad to see some girls, Virgie, Irene, Elouise, and Ruth, who had been my classmates at Webster High School. I met three girls from Gibsland, Mary, Marguerite, and Dorothy Mae, and we became roommates.

During our freshman year, there were four assigned to a room. The four of us had no problem studying and respecting the rights of others. We also spent leisure time playing a card game called "Bid Whiz". After the freshman year, there were only two people assigned to a room in the dormitory.

The Dean of Women emphasized that we become sophisticated young women. On Sundays, we had to get "dressed up" for dinner in the cafeteria. On Sundays, we wore our best dresses. Sunday evenings, we had Vesper services. Not only did we wear our best dresses, we wore hats also. The men would get "dressed up" on Sundays too. They wore suits and neckties.

I learned to appreciate opera and other cultural activities. Through lyceum attractions, I met Marion Anderson, Dr. Proctor, Dr. Benjamin Mayes, Roland Hayes, and other personalities.

For the student newspaper, my journalism class had to interview personalities who came to Southern University to perform. I was privileged to be one of a group to interview Roland Hayes.

Each year, President Felton G. Clark emphasized Founder's Day. The Founder's Day program was in memory of Dr. Joseph and Mrs. Clark, and others who played a part in organizing Southern University in Baton Rouge.

Southern University in Baton Rouge is a beautiful campus located near the banks of the Mississippi River. Students could walk down near the river, sit down and study, or socialize with their special person, as they watched "Ole Man" river roll along without a care in the world.

Buses were provided to carry girls, living in the dormitories, shopping in Baton Rouge on Tuesday, Thursday, and Saturday afternoons. Buses were also provided for those who wanted to attend church services on Sundays.

Young men visiting the young women dormitories could stay during visiting hours until 9:30 p.m. Visitations would be limited to the living room. At 9:30, they had to return to their dormitories. The thought of co-ed dorms were out of the question in the 1950's.

Finally, May, 1954 arrived and I graduated from Southern University. Having received my diploma, with clothes already packed, my mother, who came to see me graduate, and I boarded the train to North Louisiana.

Three important events that brought happiness to me in 1954 were:

1. I graduated from Southern University.
2. My son was born.
3. My son's father's tour of the U.S. Military service was completed.

Having completed his military duty, my son's father went to Southern University in

Baton Rouge to pursue his education. I remained in Cullen. After a few months, we realized that we had different goals in life, therefore, we dissolved our relationship and went our separate ways.

Having spent the first two years of my son's life home with him, I was ready to begin my career.

When the Time is Right, Move On

CHAPTER 8

Jim Dandy, The Cement Finisher

One day I was walking down Main Street in Springhill and I saw a man on his knees spreading cement on the sidewalk. I recognized him because he had shared comic books with my brother and me, when we were teenagers. He was eight years older than I was. He said, "Hello", and I said, "Hello". Then he said, "Do you need any money?" I responded very rudely, "I don't need your money", and I strutted on down the street. When I finished shopping, I stopped by John Hughes' grocery store where my friend Skeeter was working. I told her what Jim Dandy had said to me and how I responded. She said, "Fool, he is a nice person and he is not married to anyone. You know you don't have any money." That part was true; I did not have money. Actually, when Skeeter's uncle was not in the store, she would give me several cans of pet milk once or twice a week for my son. I was too proud to ask my son's father for support. He would have only had to pay five dollars per month, and that was not worth the effort.   However, my parents and his parents volunteered their support.

Thus, Jim Dandy continued to solicit my friendship. We started seeing each other on a regular basis.

CHAPTER 9

TEACHING AS A CAREER

My first teaching job was at Cullen Elementary School. I worked one semester, replacing a young man who went into the U.S. Army. I taught sixth grade at the elementary school that I had attended as a child. However, the school had been renovated.

The following summer I did domestic work at Central Baptist Church in Springhill. I did not have any problem finding a babysitter for my son. My father's sister, Aunt Lura volunteered to keep him while I worked. She did a fantastic job teaching him how to do things, getting along with other children, and developing good morals.

In September of the same year, I was employed by Webster Parish School System to teach English and social studies at Charles Brown High School in Springhill, Louisiana. I remained at Charles Brown High School teaching English for the next twelve years. It was exciting to teach there, because I had also been a high school graduate of that school.

For more than two decades, Charles Brown High School stood as a center of learning in our community, parish and state. Hundreds of students have gone out from the school to take their places in colleges, vocational schools, and schools of all occupations. The records of achievements which they have left behind and the measures of success that they have achieved, indicate that Charles Brown High School was an institution of learning of which any community would have been proud.

Students at Charles Brown High School participated and excelled in LIALO activities, which gave them the opportunity to compete in music, speech, debates, industrial arts, and sports with other students in the state of Louisiana.

The school was approved by the Southern Association of Colleges and Secondary Schools.

During my teaching career at Charles Brown High School, great strides in educational achievements and accomplishments were made under the administration of John T. Coleman, principal.

During the 1969-70 school year, the judge ordered a plan for the integration of Springhill schools. There was a district movement in the 1960's to enhance integration and to make it a reality. Meetings were held and studies were done to plan for this transitional period, whereas, the most satisfying procedures could be utilized. Many forms of integration were attempted, such as "Freedom of Choice", which some students attempted, but they were not satisfied as time passed.

Then, the "real day" arrived for students at Charles Brown High School to leave their "home school" and transfer to Springhill High School, a predominately "White" school. It was a sad day for many students and some teachers. The principal, John T. Coleman, escorted the high school students and seventeen faculty members to the new school.

Donald Curry, the president of Charles Brown High School Student Council delivered the acceptance speech on February 5, 1970. His acceptance speech is as follows: "To the Faculty and Students of Springhill High School: We appreciate the manner in which you are receiving us into your midst. We realize that these are difficult times for you, just as they are for us.

When we made the choice to become a part of this school, it was with the knowledge that we have much to offer as well as much to gain.

We want the same thing that you want, quality education. By working together, we can prove that quality is possible in a unitary system. You have shown us that you have the heart. Let us show you that we have the head."

Books, equipment, and teaching materials were transferred from Charles Brown High School to Springhill High School, a school that I could not attend as a high school student due to segregation.

Teaching at Springhill High School was interesting as well as a challenge. It afforded me the opportunity to have the experience of working in an integrated school.

It was not unusual for me to be placed on the Commencement Committee since I was one of the senior class sponsors. However, it was unusual that I had no input in the planning of the activities. I was informed by the chairperson that the Commencement program would be just as it was the year before. Even though, I agreed, I had no idea what the program was like the year before.

The time arrived for the seniors to practice for the order in which they would march into the stadium. Since I did not have anything to do with the planning of the program, I chose not to go stand in the hot sun to help students get in line for the March into the stadium. It is interesting to see how one's attitude, without voicing an opinion, can influence others. Black students got together and decided that they would get at the end of the line. The principal, who appeared to be somewhat upset, came to me and said, "The Black students are getting at the end of the line, and I have told them that they can get anywhere in line, and I do not want any repercussion from the Black community". My reply was, "I am sure that they heard what you said, and I have no control over the Black community".

Thus, graduation was over, and so was the school year.

When the Time is Right, Move On

CHAPTER 10

THE CIVIL RIGHTS MOVEMENT

The Civil Right's Movement played a very important part in America's history. As a matter of fact, the African American Civil Rights Movement became the main domestic issue in the United States during the early 1960's. Blacks joined by Whites staged demonstrations in order to express their demands for rights and equality.

My brother John, who was studying to become a lawyer, and six other law students were the first African American students to stage a demonstration at Kress Department Store lunch counter in Baton Rouge, Louisiana. Since the waitresses did not know what to do about serving African Americans, they called their manager. The manager called the policemen who placed the students in jail. They remained in jail a few hours and were later released due to the assistance of some of the local Civil Rights leaders. As a result of this event, lunch counters became integrated in Louisiana.

One of the highlights of the Civil Rights Movement came on August 28, 1963, when more than 200,000 people staged a freedom march called "March on Washington" in Washington, D.C. This event was organized by the late Civil Rights leader, Dr. Martin Luther King, Jr.

John F. Kennedy, who became President of the United States in 1961, urged Congress to pass legislation outlawing discrimination on the basis of race.

President Kennedy was killed by an assassin on November 22, 1963. Vice President Lyndon B. Johnson became the President. He persuaded Congress to pass major Civil Rights laws.

The Civil Rights Act of 1964 outlawed discrimination in employment, public accommodations, and voter registration.

When I became eligible to vote, I had to interpret part of an article that was taken from the constitution. The voter registration workers presented the articles that had been cut in parts, not necessarily at the beginning of a paragraph, and required people to interpret them. If the interpretation was not what the registration worker wanted, the person would be denied registration. Many people in the community were denied the privilege to vote because they were unable to interpret an article that had been cut in half. I probably would not have interpreted the article, if I had not had a recent course in government.

The Civil Rights Act was designed to end discrimination in the sale and renting of housing. Congress, at President Johnson's urging, also provided financial aid for the needy as part of a program called "War on Poverty".

Prior to 1968, I went to a Webster Parish Fair and completed a form at a booth where a lot for a house was being given away. A few weeks later, I received a letter from a company in Mississippi congratulating me for winning the lot. At the close of the letter, the following words were written: Restricted to White Race Only. Even though, I did not receive the lot, the Civil Rights Movement brought about many changes in America.

When the Time is Right, Move On

CHAPTER 11

THAT'S LIFE

Archie, referred to as Jim Dandy, and I dated five years and we got married in 1960. It appeared that Archie was inclined to have accidents. He was involved in a very serious automobile accident that killed his best friend, Elijah. He remained in the hospital several weeks recovering from his accident.

A few years later, he had another serious accident. He was riding a motorcycle and ran into a truck. His leg was broken in this accident. Since he was unable to work for several weeks, the owner of the truck garnisheed my check for payment of the damage that was done to the truck. Thus, there was not a dull moment in our lives. We were both happy that he recovered from that accident.

As a cement finisher, he had a good income which enabled us to buy a brick ranch style home and new mediterranean furniture. We both had our means of transportation. Therefore, we had the material things that we wanted and we were happy.

Outside forces can interfere with one's happiness, and it did interfere with ours.

Archie was a very talkative, kind and caring person. He was an excellent stepfather for my son.

His interests, drinking scotch on weekends, gambling with dice, and proclivity for women were detrimental to our relationship. Some of his buddies would tease and tell him that he could not do certain thing because he was married to a schoolteacher. He was determined to show them that he could do what he wanted to do, and so he did.

My son and I would go to church every Sunday. One Easter Sunday, at church, my son and I were dressed to the "ninth". Up walks this little girl who said to me, "My mother said to tell you that my daddy did not buy me an Easter dress." "Who is your daddy?" I asked. She said, "Archie Thomas". I responded angrily, "Hell, tell your mother that he did not buy mine either, but I am wearing one." Here I was using profanity on the church ground on an Easter Sunday morning. Outside forces continued to interfere and our relationship grew worse. Therefore, separation and eventually divorce were inevitable.

In the meantime, I met someone who showed me the bright lights and big city. I realized that life for me was far from being over.

I continued to teach at Charles Brown High School and later at Springhill High School.

Having received a NDEA grant for the 1970-71 school year, I took a sabbatical leave from the Webster Parish School System and attended the University of Central Arkansas in Conway. I completed the requirements which certified me to teach in the elementary schools with a Master's degree in Early Childhood Education.

During that year in Conway, I would go home to Cullen on weekends. That was my son's last year in high school, and he was living with my mother. I knew it was necessary for me to check his progress as well as the progress of other members of the family.

Also, during that year in Conway, I met the aspiring Dr. John Greene, as he called himself. We developed a unique relationship that had an influence on my life.

My graduation from the University of Central Arkansas occurred two weeks before my son's graduation from high school. I had to make the most difficult decision of my life. That was to put space between me and my hometown or miss my son's high school graduation. I did not attend his high school graduation, but I was there for his graduation from Louisiana Tech University, Southern Illinois University-Edwardsville, and other important events in his life. The time was right and I moved on to improve my life.

Upon graduation from the University of Central Arkansas, my desire was to leave Louisiana, and John Greene's desire was to leave Arkansas. Therefore, we headed for Washington, D.C. by way of Cleveland. My intention was to spend two weeks with my brother, who was an attorney with Ohio Bell Telephone Company, and continue to Washington, D.C. to get a job teaching.

My brother suggested that I get a job teaching in the Cleveland area. I looked in the telephone directory and started writing different school systems for application forms. I submitted quite a few. The first job offer I received was in the Berea School System. I went for an interview and was hired. I was thrilled to get the job. I quickly resigned from teaching in the Webster Parish School System.

In the meantime, John Greene had aspirations of getting a job in the medical field. He was interviewed at every hospital in Cleveland, but he did not qualify for the position that he wanted.

Therefore, he became a free-lance photographer. The relationship with John Greene ended five years later. I appreciate him for teaching me to "stand on my own two feet" and depend strictly on myself. Again, the time was right and I moved on to a better place in my life.

George Buck, Jr. and I were very good friends throughout the years that I had been in Cleveland. He was the first person that I knew who could organize a new business and do well. We communicated with each other every day. That is why it was so unusual on one weekend in June of 1989, I telephoned him on Friday night, Saturday and Sunday, and only received the message on his answering machine. Later Sunday morning, I received a telephone call from one of his friends. She asked me if he were dead. I said, "No!" She said that there is an article in today's Plain Dealer. I had read the newspaper, but I did not see that article. I called the morgue to verify his death. He had been killed Friday night by a drunken woman driver in a head-on collision. I had a book with the telephone numbers of his brothers, sister, and niece. I had the sad job of informing them about his death.

His brother and sister-in-law from Chicago came to Cleveland, and Buck's body was sent to his hometown in Mississippi for burial. I flew down to Mississippi and attended the funeral. It is sad for me to lose a friend.

My mother and I had planned a trip to Hawaii. Four days after Buck's funeral, we were flying to Hawaii. I went through the process of doing every thing that we had on our agenda. My mother said that she enjoyed our vacation. I would have enjoyed it more, had I not been sad about the loss of my friend.

Well, thinking of the year 1978, even though we were divorced, Archie and I had made an agreement that whoever died first, he or I, that the surviving one would see that the deceased was buried in an elegant manner.

Thus, on a Saturday morning in December of 1978, my son, Dwayne, called from St. Louis and said, "Mur, Pop is dead." I said, "Who?" He said, "Pop, Archie Thomas". He had a heart attack while working on the job at International Paper Mill. Therefore, I took a flight to Louisiana to make sure that our agreement would be done. When I arrived, Archie's brother from Texas had made the arrangement with Memorial Funeral Home. He informed me that I would like what he had chosen. I said, "ok fine". The following day, he came to me and said, "I just came from International Paper Company, and his insurance is made out to you. You will be getting the money to use for whatever you choose." Well, one choice was to pay for the burial expenses that I had no part in selecting, and I did pay the expenses.

The funeral was held at First Baptist Church in Cullen, Louisiana with friends and relatives attending the service. Elder Jonathan Washington presented the eulogy. Thus, the last of the "Big Time Spenders", as he referred to himself, was buried in the Garden of Memory Cemetery.

I can appreciate the people in my life and those who were once a part of my life. Each one brought a different experience and a lesson to be learned that influenced my life. Each experience enabled me to grow into the person who I am today.

CHAPTER 12

SELF IMPROVEMENT

In an effort to be well informed of the changes in education, I attended workshops that the Berea School District provided for teachers. To better understand emerging adolescents, I enrolled in a graduate program at Cleveland State University and received a second Master's Degree. This degree was in Curriculum Foundation with emphasis on the emerging adolescent. These experiences enabled me to do an effective job of teaching children 23 years in the Berea School System.

With an accumulation of 37 teaching years, I retired from the Berea City School District in 1994. The time was right for me to move on to a different aspiration.

Having taught in schools with predominately African American students and predominately Caucasian students, I have found that if the following conditions exist: good support, good instruction, motivation, high expectation, and commitment, all children should succeed.

Having retired from teaching, I have a seasonal job with a photography company. The following poem gives a description.

ALL IN A DAY'S WORK

We rush, rush, rush
The cameras are taken down.
The equipment is loaded
Into a company van

We drive, drive, drive,
From schools across the state
Back to the studio
The equipment is unloaded,
And placed into a bin.

Cashiers make a run
For the tabulation room.
We rush, rush, rush,
To get our work done.
We do not dare
Keep photographers waiting.

Rush, drive, tabulate,
Where will it lead us?
To a lovely photograph, I speculate.
When day is over, work is done.
That is the perfect picture of a day.

One day near the end of the century,
A system was created,
That we all appreciated.
No more despair at the end of a day.
That is the perfect picture of a day.

FAMOUS WORDS AND WISDOM

"If you play with fire, you'll get burnt".
                    Grandmother Allie Hunter

"A poor wind that never changes." "Nothing beats a failure but a try."
                    Great Grandmother Isabell Johnson

"Help him, Lord, help him".
                    Great Grandmother Mary Ann Hunter

"You doggone come a jumping."
                    Grand Daddy Hunter

"They are taking the rag off the bush." "They are gone some place to pull a stunt."

Grandfather Will Johnson

"If you can't say something nice about a person, don't say anything."

Grandmother Olelia T. Johnson

"Don't involve anyone else in your mess."

Mother Altee Johnson

"There are two sides to a problem."

Daddy Felton Johnson

"Mur, the Lord will provide."
                                    Son-Dwayne Buggs

"Let us pray."
                                    Pastor B.J. Epps

"He can who thinks he can."
                                    John T. Coleman, Principal

"They might beat us playing basketball tonight, but they won't be any 'sharper' than we are."
                                    Principal Charles H. Brown

"One trip."

Robert (Son) Valentine

"We at Brown High School work hard and we play hard."

James Rhynes

"We thank God for each account of yesterday and take courage for tomorrow."

Betty Rhynes

"Girl, you look while I drive."

W.M. Presley

"I know that's right because I have a book with that in it."

Arletha Miles

"I wrote you a letter, but my mother did not give it to you."

O.J. Buggs

"When the grass starts growing, folks start lying."
Grandmother A. Hunter

"That's an evil place with evidence of antichrist."
J. Johnson

"I am doing all right for an old man."

K. Sullivan

"I thought I remembered the personality, but I can't remember from whence it came."

Mergie Presley

"I'll be here (at First Baptist) until Tom Tanken comes."

Rev. A.W. Grant

"I know that's true because I saw it with these eyes."

Margaret Grant

"Mur, you should not wear those fancy hats to church; people look at you instead of looking at the preacher."

Dwayne Buggs

"As I learn better, I do better."

Rev. J. Washington

"I'll tell it like it is."

L. Rhone

"Lord, bless us all."

Mother Hunter

"I knew you were coming."
Daddy Hunter

"My friend said, 'Don't sweat the small stuff'."
Margaret Redmond

"No one has a corner on education."
Marilyn Okoye

"You are a good looking ole Indian woman."
J. Greene

"Hey Babe, do you know who loves you?"

J. Wasp

"I'll love you until they throw dirt into my face."

W.J. Jones

"I'm glad to hear your little sweet voice."

C.J. Edwards

"I am the last of the big time spenders."

A.T. Thomas

"...Don't ever be without a car."

J. Morris

"If you talk all the time, you don't have time to listen."

Jodie Sims

"They promised and didn't do it, so I am going to tell them about that."

Emma Sims

"I didn't have anyone else to talk to about this, so I waited to talk to you."

Mother Altee Johnson

"When my ship comes in…" "…a pain, but Lord, please don't move that pain."

V. Renty

"Don't worry about me, I'll be all right".

I. Mackey

"Can I help it if I am cute in the face, neat in the waist, and have great big legs?"

Allie M. Nelams

"You all know that it is not right to go to the show on Sundays."

E. Davis Brooks

"How is my favorite sister?"

M. Thomas

"...I definitely know...

Fred D. Williams

"We are all born equal."

Mary Hollo

"I am already on a committee."

Chris Geniusz

"Put in three big ones."

Ron Geniusz

"Follow your heart."

M. Okoye

"That's more than a notion."

Leroy Campbell

"We cooked this pie because the baby liked it."

Loretta Grady

"Faye, I am going to this interview with you and Genieve to make sure that both of you get accepted."

Mildred Q. Johnson

"Look your best when you walk out; you never know who you might meet."

Magaline Quarles

"Let me tell you how I did that…"

L. Radford

"I am as good as anybody."

M. Underwood

"I don't need anyone to pull me down, I can go down by myself."

Ike Adams

"Well, you see, it's like this…"

H. Rhone, Sr.

"You can stand there saying your valedictorian speech and sound country if you want to."

Lillian Graham Chapman

"… I can tell the difference when I am wearing a hundred dollar dress."

Ruth White

Speaking to football players, "… son, your mama could do better."

Al Dennis

"We are not communicating."

F. Thomas

"How you all doing up there?"

Rosie Smith

"Brother Pastor, that deacon over there is no good."

Margaret Coleman

"You are not like me, I would pull up every one those corn plants that she planted in my yard."

Aunt Lura Owens

"I hope no one I know sees me looking like this."

Aunt Clotee Ridley

Looking in address book, "Who do I know in this town?"

Aunt Esther Nelson

Speaking to grandson, "Come on in out of that hot sun before it turns you…"

Cleara Mae Buggs

"Let me tell you about Mr. Hard Time."

Bessie Robinson

Dwayne's First Hat

Faye and Overton Joe

Archie Thomas, Alma Salter and Faye J. Thomas Charles Brown High School Senior Prom

Faye J. Thomas
Charles Brown High School Staff
English Department

Geneva Jackson and Faye J. Thomas
Charles H. Brown High School
Springhill, Louisiana

Faye Johnson Thomas, Felton Johnson, Clotee Johnson Ridley, Esther Johnson Nelson and Dwayne A. Buggs.

**Rita Murphy Johnson, John W. Johnson, Sr.
and Altee Hunter Johnson
Wedding at Shadowbrook
New Jersey**

**Esther Johnson Nelson and CloteeJohnson
Ridley
Detroit, Michigan**

John Johnson, Jr.

Lura Johnson Owens, Esther Johnson Nelson, Faye Johnson Thomas, Gunn, Clotee Johnson Ridley Park near Chicago, Illinois.

**Clotee Ridley, esther Nelson, Faye J. Thomas,
Allie Hunter and Altee Johnson**

Altee H. Johnson and Dwayne A. Buggs
Springhill, Louisiana
Civic Center Park

Alteee Johnson and Grandsons:
Julian W. Johnson and Juan W. Johnson
Law School Graduation
Baton Rouge, Louisiana.

**Altee Hunter Johnson and Faye Johson Thomas
In Hawaii**

Faye J. Thomas, Charles Renty and Virgie Renty.

**Cleo Cage, Norma Cage, Altee Johnson and
Faye J. Thomas.**

**Charles Brown Society Annual Program
Springhill Civic Center.**

Faye J. Thomas and Pete Harris
Freeman and Harris Café
Shreveport, Louisiana

Altee Johnson and John W. Johnson, Sr.
Fellowship Baptist Church
Lillie, Louisiana

Retirement Banquet
Holiday Inn—Middleburg Heights, Ohio
Honoree Faye J. Thomas and Family
1994

About the Author

Faye Evelyn Johnson Thomas, a retired schoolteacher, was born in Summerfield, Louisiana. She grew up in Cullen, Louisiana, a small paper mill town. She now resides in Middlesburg Heights, Ohio, a southwestern suburb of Cleveland.

Her son, Dwayne, an educator in music, lives in St. Louis, Missouri.

Faye graduated from Southern University in Baton Rouge, Louisiana, with a major in English and a minor in Social Studies. She was the recipient of a 1969-70 NDEA grant, which enabled her to obtain a MSE degree in Early Childhood Education from the University of Central Arkansas in Conway, Arkansas. In 1979, she received a Master of Education degree in Curricular Foundation from Cleveland State University in Cleveland, Ohio. She was also a 1984-85 Jennings Scholar.

Her autobiographical sketch is listed in *Who's Who in the Midwest, Who's Who in American Education, Who's Who in America,* and *The Biographical Roll of Honor.*

Her poetry has been included in the anthologies *America at the Millennium* and *Poetry's Elite.*

She is a member of Antioch Baptist Church in Cleveland, and a CTM of Midpark Toastmasters.

Printed in the United States
1087400002B

9 780759 669475